No Judgment

Caitlin Press Inc.
3375 Ponderosa Way
Qualicum Beach, BC V9K 2J8
www.caitlinpress.com

Text and cover design by Vici Johnstone
Printed in Canada

Quote on pages 23-24 used with permission from CBC Licensing

Caitlin Press Inc. acknowledges financial support from the Government of Canada and the Canada Council for the Arts, and the Province of British Columbia through the British Columbia Arts Council and the Book Publisher's Tax Credit.

Canada Council   Conseil des Arts   BRITISH COLUMBIA   Funded by the   Canada
for the Arts   du Canada   ARTS COUNCIL   Government
                                                        of Canada

No judgment : and other busking stories / by Philip Seagram.
Seagram, Philip, author.
Canadiana 20240466586 | ISBN 9781773861616 (softcover)
LCSH: Seagram, Philip. | LCSH: Singers—Canada—Biography. | LCSH: Street musicians—Canada—Biography. | LCSH: Judges—British Columbia—Biography. | LCGFT: Autobiographies.
LCC ML420.S438 A3 2025 | DDC 782.42164092—dc23

No Judgment

And Other Busking Stories

Philip Seagram

CAITLIN PRESS 2025

Author's Note

The stories in this book are true; the people in them are real. To protect their privacy I have changed the appearance of some of these people, or the location where I met them.

For Dana, who had a hand in this too.

Contents

Jump — 9

The Sign — 18

Willie Thrasher — 21

Lethbridge — 25

No Judgment — 28

Wagon Wheel — 36

AM Radio — 42

Metro — 48

Fredericton and St. John — 54

Hot Dogs — 59

Police Lake — 68

Small Things — 77

After — 82

Acknowledgments — 93

About the Author — 95

Jump

The first time I try busking, a woman, mature and well dressed, approaches and stands about four feet in front of me. With a serious face she waits patiently until I finish the song.

"What are you doing?" she asks.

I have just been asking myself the same thing. It is late November in Toronto, early afternoon, and I've been playing continuously for over an hour. I am set up on Yonge Street, near the exit of a pharmacy. The wind is driving hail horizontally down the city's spine to Lake Ontario. People are moving quickly along the sidewalk before me, heads down, hunched against the elements. Despite my long underwear, toque and fingerless gloves, I am freezing. I can barely find any chords with my left hand and can feel nothing with the fingers of my right hand. I am just flailing with it, trying to sing over the crude sounds I am able to bring out of the guitar. With the traffic noise, the construction less than half a block away and the constant general din of the city, I've been wondering if anyone can hear my acoustic contribution anyway. I might be the only busker in all of Toronto at this moment, and for good reason.

That morning I had fashioned a sign from an empty cardboard box. With a black Sharpie I had scrawled: "I'm playing for fun! Please: Leave what you want, Take what you need, and have a great day!" Just the right tone, I thought. Cheerful. Positive.

Given the conditions on Yonge Street this afternoon, however, the sign clearly lacks credibility, and probably suggests outright fraud. The woman who is asking what I am doing obviously isn't convinced. She stands there waiting for a response, the hail catching in the greying hair framing her face under a hand-knit beret. I realize I don't have a good answer, or at least not one that makes any sense. I give her the most truthful answer I can.

"I'm… practising," I say.

She looks at me closely, more than a hint of worry now on her face.

Some explanation is necessary.

On a Sunday evening one year before my busking baptism, I stood at the raised computer station in my office in Nelson, reading and re-reading the email I'd just composed, occasionally turning away from the screen to look through the tall window to my right. This had been my view for many Sundays over the previous five years, through the chestnut trees growing along the near sidewalk, out across Vernon Street with its boulevard bearing flower beds and a statue of God-knows-what, to the understated entrance of the Hume Hotel on the other side.

November is a gloomy time of year in Nelson. The days are short, the fall colours gone, the snow line creeping down the mountainside. The trees outside my office window that night stood dark and leafless. A month earlier I'd picked up a few chestnuts from the sidewalk as I entered the building and laid them on the corner of my desk. They'd since lost their lustre and were slowly shrinking as they dried out, but for years it had been my habit to place fresh chestnuts there until the next year's crop fell from the trees. I don't know exactly why.

As was usual on weekends, I was the only person in the cavernous courthouse, my office an oasis of warm light amongst the dark corridors and creaking staircases. I had spent most of the day reviewing the family court cases scheduled for the next day. There were dozens of them, each with its own miserable history of conflict. The files, some more than six inches thick, now stood upright on a large trolley beside my desk, the neat rows belying the chaotic contents of their accordion folders. In the morning a clerk would retrieve the cart and wheel it into the courtroom, like a stretcher bearing the wounded into a frontline triage unit.

I read the email again: "After much careful thought I have decided to leave my position..." etc. I was stalling, realizing that all that was left was one click of a mouse. I had the feeling of standing on a high cliff, looking down at the surface of a lake, wondering at how very small and distant the waves below look.

I don't remember exactly where I was, or even exactly what day it was, when the idea of leaving, one that had brewed in my mind for months, finally became a decision. Once made, it sat with me, constantly on my mind. I lived with it for a week or two, maybe a month, thinking I might wake up one morning and find it gone or replaced by some other option, but this didn't happen. If anything, the decision became heavier and more insistent, a hulking presence demanding action.

So, that Sunday night in my office, I acted. I breathed in, moved the cursor over "Send," and whispered "Jump" as I clicked.

ʎ

When you jump off a cliff there is a feeling of weightlessness, then of rapid acceleration and motion culminating in the impact with the surface of the water. While there is a sort of time-altered, slow-motion feeling to the experience, it's all over pretty quickly. Before you know it you are swimming for the surface and heading for the shore, yelling adrenalin-charged encouragement up to the next person waiting at the cliff's edge. When you leap from a cliff there are no opportunities to change your mind and turn back.

Not so the process of leaving a career. When I got out of court the next afternoon I found an email from the Chief Judge waiting for me. Would I please call her at my earliest convenience? I would and I did. That call was followed by a series of calls and emails with one of the Associate Chief Judges, in turn followed by an awkward call from the judge who chaired the judicial wellness committee. Was I all right? Had I thought this through? Did I need some time off? Did I need to talk to someone? Let's give it a few months and see if your feelings change, shall we? And so it went. All very well meant and tactfully put, yet carrying the implicit message that I was making a mistake, that I was doing the wrong thing, that I should reconsider. After all, I was not quite sixty (young for a judge to retire), doing meaningful work well and earning a comfortable living. I had a good fifteen years left in my career.

I had given seven months' notice. Those were long months. Once word of my intended departure got out, I started getting calls and emails from colleagues. Most of these were along the same lines—polite inquiries as to the state of my health, physical or otherwise, some a little more blunt ("What's going on?").

Other messages and conversations were different, though. Some of my colleagues expressed admiration and encouragement, even envy. Still, I grew tired of explaining myself. I resented having to justify my decision. As the months dragged on, every time I was called on to lay out my reasons for leaving, my resolve to follow through on the decision was reinforced until, as in that moment when you leap off the cliff, there was no question of turning back. Finally, my last day of judging came and went.

Where does the busking come in? As that last judging day approached, I had begun to think I needed to do something to mark the end of this part of my life, to put some distance between it and me, to help me disengage. I wanted to go somewhere and do something simple and hard. I had clichéd visions of walking the Camino in Spain, or hiking the Pacific Crest Trail from Mexico to Canada. A friend suggested kayaking from Alaska to Vancouver. As I mulled these possibilities over, the idea of travelling across Canada and playing guitar and singing on city streets as I went began to take shape. I'd never been across Canada, and it felt wrong that I had never been to Winnipeg, or Saskatoon, or Moncton, or Charlottetown or many other Canadian cities. Busking provided a reason to travel, a purpose, a unique way to experience a place. And for me, a relatively novice musician—and one who had never played on the street before—a busking trip represented a real challenge, a step well outside my comfort zone.

I had hoped to begin this trip immediately after my last day on the bench. But the travel restrictions imposed by the Covid pandemic, still in full swing in the spring of 2021, prevented that. Compelled to stay busy, I filled the months that followed with other pursuits: building a carport, releasing an EP with the band I had been in for several years, volunteering for a local non-profit organization, working as a cross-country ski instructor through the winter. I was struggling with the novelty of free time and was doing everything I could to avoid it. I kept myself busy, but the idea of a trip across Canada stayed on my mind.

By the spring of 2022, the country had begun to emerge from the pandemic. Travelling, carefully, began to be possible. By then I had begun to envision the trip as more than just a way of sealing the end of the career I had left a year earlier. I had in mind a chautauqua journey of the kind described in Robert Pirsig's *Zen and the Art of Motorcycle Maintenance*. An opportunity to work on overcoming the self-consciousness I felt when performing. A time to think, to have open, uninterrupted time, to reflect, assess and take stock. A journey. A challenge. An adventure.

But the reasons for taking this trip across Canada were not well thought out; in hindsight they were more likely rationalizations, pat justifications or hopeful aspirations. They were what I told myself at the time. From where I am now, it seems I wanted to get out there without knowing exactly why.

Back to Yonge Street and the curious woman outside the pharmacy. It was November 2021, five months since I'd left my job, and I was in Toronto visiting my mother for a week. I'd brought my guitar on the trip because it's hard for me to go a day without playing it. By then I'd been thinking about the busking trip for almost a year without any knowledge of what busking was actually like. For some reason, most likely the need to escape the house and my mother's company for a bit, that morning I decided to test the waters I'd been thinking about for so long.

There is an implicit request in busking. The open guitar case on the sidewalk is clear in what it asks for. Money for music; there's nothing wrong in that. But even without ever having done it I felt that busking was different from a gig in a bar or a farmers' market. When busking, the musician puts themself into others' lives uninvited. To me at the time it seemed more like hawking, or one step up from panhandling, and I was uncomfortable with this. This notion now seems silly to me, a feeling maybe born of phony pride or unacknowledged false assumptions about people who busk, but at the time, there it was. So, partly to soften this discomfort, I drew up the cardboard sign that invited both giving and taking. But the two-sided invitation was appealing to me for other reasons as well. Years before, I'd seen a news article about a musician doing this in subway stations somewhere in the USA, and I remember feeling lifted by it. The idea of offering music as a backdrop for others to act with blind generosity, like paying one's luck forward or committing random acts of kindness, was unusual and refreshing. There was something inherently hopeful about it. I wanted to be part of something like this, even on the smallest of scales.

So off I went, taking the subway up to Yonge and Davisville, grabbing a coffee and setting up in the recessed area near the pharmacy exit. Hitting that first chord and pushing those first few sung words out of my mouth was another jump, a big one, and an hour and a half later the concerned woman was asking me what I was doing. I'd been throwing my voice and guitar out into the wind and hail and constant motion and commotion of the sidewalk and the street and I was frozen, exhausted. There were a few coins in my guitar case, and a ten-dollar bill that at the time I reasoned had been placed there more out of sympathy than appreciation. No one had taken any money out. I was shaking from the cold, but also from exhilaration—not the same as one feels from jumping off a cliff into water, but there nonetheless. In that first session I had tasted the sense of freedom that the anonymity of playing on the street can bring. I felt vulnerable and powerful. And I had learned something already:

people may ignore or pretend to ignore a busker as they pass by, but they will always, even surreptitiously, read the sign the busker puts out.

At an Asian fusion restaurant just down the street from where I'd been playing, I spent eighteen dollars—three more than I'd made playing—on a pot of green tea and a bowl of wonton soup. I wrapped my fingers around both steaming vessels, finding profound satisfaction in the pins and needles of returning circulation. The busking trip across Canada, until that day an idea, a hypothetical, had become a commitment. There was no question I was going to do it once the winter passed. What I had said to the good woman was true. I *was* practising.

The Sign

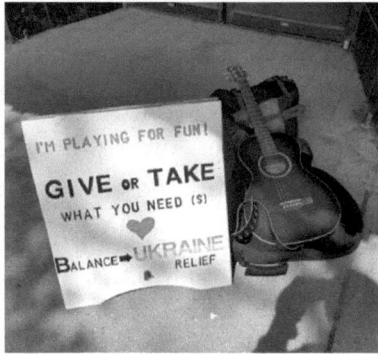

I decided, with my now-firm determination to take this cross-country busking trip, I would need a proper sign, something more than a ragged piece of cardboard with some scrawled writing on it. I realized that the sign would have to inspire trust, to draw people in. So I put a fair bit a of work into it, digging through my scraps of plywood, measuring and cutting the pieces, sanding the surfaces and edges, buying real acrylic paint at an art supply store. What I came up with wasn't perfect, but I thought it hit the mark. It was big enough to be seen from a distance, but not aggressive. It looked like what it was—homemade— but carefully so. Full disclosure: my wife, dear Dana, drew in the heart.

By April 2022, Russia had invaded Ukraine. The war was two months old and the people of Kyiv were living in underground subway stations as missiles rained on their city. Civilians were fleeing the country. My older sister, who lives in a small apartment in southern France, was taking in Ukrainian refugees as they made their way to safety. Like her and many others, I wanted to do something about the war, and thus hatched the idea of adding fundraising for Ukraine humanitarian relief to the give/take dynamic.

I paid attention to the legal niceties of each city I played in, paranoid about finding myself at the mercy of some over-zealous enforcement officer and having my guitar confiscated or, worse, landing on some amused judge's morning docket. As it turned out, the most restrictive busking laws in the whole country are where I started, in Victoria. The Victoria bylaws on "street entertainment" are detailed and extensive. There are rules about where, when and how one may perform. There is even a separate section of the bylaw devoted to the regulation of the public playing of bagpipes (fair enough!). All buskers must complete a detailed application form and purchase a licence in person at city hall. A successful application will result in the issuance of an official badge engraved with the street entertainer's licence number. The badge must be worn at all times during a performance. *The romantic autonomy of the busker takes a hit*, I thought as I read the bylaw, but what really caught my attention was the section that said that only signage approved by the city could be displayed. This worried me. My sign was crucial.

On the first morning of the trip I walked into Victoria City Hall as soon as the doors were unlocked. The woman behind the reception counter was, happily, far less intimidating than her city's bylaws. She cheerfully processed my application, took my money and handed me a neon yellow badge. At that point I mentioned my sign, which I'd brought to the counter with me. She eyed it in a non-committal way. "Signs aren't allowed unless approved by the bylaw officers," she said, and told me where their office was.

It was a short walk to the bylaw enforcement office, where the door was locked. I knocked, and a uniformed officer came to the door, coffee in hand. An older guy, he bore the tired expression of someone who'd spent a career dealing with upset people and was counting the days to retirement. I showed him the sign. He glanced at it and said, "I can't approve it. It's too big. It'll take up too much space and the businesses won't like it." Then I could see him actually reading it. I quickly told him how I would stand it so it straddled my guitar case and wouldn't take up any additional space, and how I intended to find a spot where I wouldn't obstruct anyone's path. I also promised to remove the sign if anyone complained. Deal.

Off I went then, with my approved sign, to set up and play in Victoria's Bastion Square. I wasn't completely law-abiding, however. Although I had it with me, stowed in my guitar case, I could not bring myself to wear the garish, city-issued badge.

In the weeks that followed, the sign, as much as my guitar, became my constant companion, a vital part of my presence on the street. It was my raison d'être, my answer to the question posed by the woman during my first busking session on Yonge Street the previous fall.

Willie Thrasher

It's a clear, cold morning on the Nanaimo waterfront. A gusting north wind scuffs the water in the harbour and rattles the stays and halyards of the sailboats. Both water and sky are a piercing, almost impossible blue. I am scouting, looking for the most promising of the three or four spots the city has designated for busking.

I come across an older Indigenous man sitting on a retaining wall at one of the spots. He is singing an early Beatles song, "I Saw Her Standing There," and playing a twelve-string that has seen a lot of miles. The man sings and strums with huge energy. His voice is raw and direct; there is nothing held back. His guitar has several broken strings hanging from the bridge. I watch and listen from a respectful distance, then put some coins down. He breaks from the song long enough to say, "Thank you," and his smile stretches wide as I carry on.

About five minutes later I am heading back past the spot and the man is on his feet, having a smoke and looking out at the harbour as he takes a break from playing. We start talking and he immediately introduces himself as Willie Thrasher. He tells me he is originally from Inuvik and played and toured across Canada for many years with a band called the Cordells. When I tell him I'm from Nelson he says he played there at the Capitol Theatre a few years ago. Now he lives in Nanaimo and busks almost every day. "People are good," he says. "The kids are the best, they get so into it."

As we're talking a man walks by, says hello to Willie Thrasher, addressing him by name, and puts a healthy handful of change on the soft guitar case still lying on the walkway. Willie Thrasher says he is going to stop playing in about twenty minutes and offers me his spot. He tells me to go get my guitar. I think to myself, this man is as he plays, open hearted.

I retrieve my guitar from my car but end up playing at another, sunnier spot on the harbour. Not long after I start playing, though, Willie Thrasher rides up on his bike and listens for a while. Then, with a wave, he peddles off.

I've since learned that Willie Thrasher was seventy-four years old when I met him. At the age of five he was taken from his family and placed in a boarding school run by the Catholic Church under the Canadian government's residential school system. He was in that system until he was sixteen. For much of the balance of his life he has used music to heal and to reclaim his cultural identity, and to help other survivors do the same.

But these scant facts tell nothing of the reality of this man's life. It deserves a book of its own.

What pushed me to learn more about Willie Thrasher was a radio interview I heard while driving through northern Ontario a little more than a month after meeting him. The winding corridor of the highway through the granite cliffs and still-frozen lakes of the Canadian Shield seemed endless. Between stretches of dead radio I could usually pick up CBC. I'd leave the radio on quietly, even if all I was getting was static, hit the scan button and wait until it picked up something, then turn it up. One morning, somewhere between Winnipeg and Thunder Bay, it picked up a man's voice. *I know that voice*, I thought, but I couldn't immediately place it. CBC's *The Sunday Magazine* was re-playing an interview with Willie Thrasher that had aired earlier in the year, just before Indigenous delegations on behalf of First Nations, Métis and Inuit in Canada were to meet the Pope in Rome to discuss the Church's part in the Canadian residential school system. The interview mostly covered Willie Thrasher's musical career and his role in the revival of Indigenous music in Canada, but toward the end it touched on the upcoming meetings with the Pope. The reporter asked Willie Thrasher what he would say to the leaders of the Catholic Church if he had a chance. Willie Thrasher said, in part:

> ...I would tell the Pope that, you know, the Great Spirit, God, has never, never once told anybody to force their traditions and beliefs inside [others]. It was passed on by God; it was given by God, and whatever each culture around the world believed, it came from God, and you cannot take that away from them. And that's what the Catholic Church did, you know. I don't blame them, I don't blame them, you

know. That's how they are, and they had so much power in Rome that they forgot Jesus. They used the words instead of love. They used something that was totally against what God has put on this earth... to teach to be together...

This was the first time I'd heard the idea that different belief systems could be given to different cultures by the same god, and it struck me as both brilliant and unassailably logical. Trust an omniscient god to avoid a one-size-fits-all strategy.

When I met Willie Thrasher that day in Nanaimo we were just two buskers exchanging a few friendly words, listening to each other's music and enjoying a crisp spring morning on the waterfront. That encounter was enough in itself. But there is more to it now, to me. There are still heroes out there, people who show us what we are capable of.

Lethbridge

There is hardly a soul on the lunch hour streets, such is the wind. The few who have ventured out lean into it, focussed entirely on bracing themselves so they do not fall. They appear not to notice me, tucked in the lee of a notch where two buildings meet unevenly, or the guitar case and sign anchored by my backpack on the margin of the sidewalk. It is sunny, but cold enough that my fingers are already stiffening. I am taking some delight in the absurdity of this scene. I fling my songs into the gale and the empty street and think of a play by Samuel Beckett.

Eventually a woman approaches and stands before the sign, studying it. I can barely see her face deep within her hoodie. She might be twenty. Overtop the hoodie she wears a windbreaker with a broken zipper. Her hands are jammed in the pockets and crossed in front of her body to wrap it to her as close as she can. "What does 'give or take' mean?" she asks. She has no front teeth. I'm still playing chords, but it doesn't matter; it can hardly be heard. I explain the sign.

The woman continues to stand there, staring into the case. The seed money is about two dollars in silver and a five-dollar bill I have secured, visibly, under a large rock. She fishes in the pocket of her sweatpants and brings out a loonie. She puts the coin in the case, lifts the stone and takes the bill. She walks on. "Have a great day," I call after her, simultaneously thinking how lame that sounds.

When the woman gets to the corner, she turns around and walks back, against the wind. "What's with Ukraine? What's that about?" she asks.

We talk about it.

I ended up, cash-wise, on the positive side that day. As I was setting up I had briefly chatted with a carpenter working in the building I was backed against. As we talked he squinted and held his forearm before his face to deflect the sting of the wind and the late-winter road grit it carried. He went out to his van at some point after my exchange with the young woman and brought back ten dollars. I don't know if he had seen the earlier incident, but I'm guessing he had.

After finishing the set I had to clean out my guitar case. A perfect, sculpted dune of sand and dust had accumulated there as I played.

A note about the weather. I started in Victoria on April 1, aware of the potential irony of that date but keen to charge ahead anyway. I had two months to get across the country and back home to Nelson. In early April, BC was fine, at least in the south, but once I left its relatively balmy realm, things took a turn. As I crossed the prairies, winter storms were rolling through. In the small towns off the highway where I stopped for coffee and food, the parking lots were bordered with mountains of piled-up snow. People were still hunkered down, their trucks gathered around nondescript cafés with opaque windows. Inside, in parkas and boots, they sat over coffee, speaking in low tones and looking up briefly when I entered, like somnolent bears checking out a newcomer to their den. In these towns, even at midday, there was no one on the street.

The wind was everywhere. As I pushed across the heaves and swells of the prairie there were times I thought my little Honda Fit, running out its old winter tires and packed with camping gear and my guitar, would be thrown off the highway. I caught myself leaning into the wind, two hands clenched in a death grip on the wheel, resisting the gusts that slammed into the car like bodychecks.

By late April I was crossing northern Ontario, also still snowbound. Lake Superior was a brooding grey presence on my right, its shores ringed with massive ice drifts. As I descended into southern Ontario and Quebec the wind lessened and the sun began to give some heat, but in northern New Brunswick people were still ice fishing on the small lakes I passed.

All of this made for tough busking conditions. In the eight weeks of the trip, there was only the rare day when, if I found a sunny spot that was sheltered from the wind, I could stay warm enough that my fingers wouldn't require regular warming between songs. Mostly it was cold out there.

In Lethbridge, within a week of starting the trip, I realized I had started this journey two months too soon. Hello, April Fool.

No Judgment

When I get to downtown Sudbury it seems unnaturally quiet, as if the Apocalypse has already come and gone, leaving just a few survivors wandering the streets. I drive around a bit, trying to get a feel for it. At the bus depot I see people sitting and milling about, but otherwise the city's core is virtually deserted. It takes a while before I remember it is Sunday.

Eventually I spot an open coffee shop with the occasional person going in and out. I decide to set up, get some practice in and enjoy playing in the warmth of the day. I put my case and sign down against an office building about thirty feet from the door to the café. Across the street is a small parking lot and other office buildings. I start playing.

People continue to trickle in and out of the coffee shop. I notice also that people are regularly entering and leaving the building I am backed against. Most are dropped off by taxis or other vehicles, and many have walkers or wheelchairs. I look more closely at the sign by the entrance and see it is a medical clinic.

People begin dropping coins, and several of them sit on a nearby bench. Two older men wearing meshed baseball caps advertising heavy equipment walk by without acknowledgment, but they both stop and stand about six feet to my left, backed against the building and looking across to the parking lot as I am, like sentries. They are upwind, and one chain-smokes flavoured cigarettes.

Two people throw five-dollar bills on top of the coins. It's adding up. There is little traffic noise to compete with and it seems we have become an attraction, or at least a curiosity, the only action taking place on these Sunday streets. I've been playing for less than an hour and I am up at least thirty dollars on top of the eight dollars of seed money I started with.

A young woman approaches and asks the man standing off to my left what "give or take" means. He gestures toward me, and I tell the woman people can leave money or take it if they need it. She says, "I need four dollars and seventy-five cents." I tell her she is free to take it, and she does, thanking me as she leaves.

I carry on playing and a few more coins come in. A woman with a walker who had previously gone into the clinic comes out and shuffles by, focussed on the sidewalk two feet in front of her. She glances at the guitar case and throws in a toonie.

"You're doing all right," she says. I agree with her and mention that some money has gone out as well. She frowns and says, "They probably don't need it."

I say, "Well, that's where the trust part comes in."

"I know," she says, moving on.

About five minutes later there is a small figure crouching in front of the case. When she looks up I see she is a youth, maybe thirteen at most, and I look for a parent or friend she might be with. There is none. The girl is tiny. She looks directly at me from within the cowl of her black hoodie. I can see her dark hair cut straight across her forehead and the heavy eyeliner extending beyond her eyes in the style of Amy Winehouse. The girl's skin is incredibly pale. She looks like an urban elf who has gotten into her mother's makeup kit. There is a bulky bag over her shoulder, and she clutches a half-eaten bagel in one hand, a Subway cup in the other.

The girl remains crouched over the case, eyeing the contents. She asks, "Does 'give or take' mean I can take money?" I tell her it does.

"How much can I take?"

"You can take what you need," I say.

"I need ten dollars." There are still only two bills in the case, the fives.

"If you need it then you can take it," I say. She seems to be hesitating, so I add, "No judgment."

"No judgment," she repeats, slowly.

The girl puts the Subway cup on the sidewalk and balances the bagel on its lid. She takes the two fives and tucks them in her pocket. Then, one-by-one, she silently picks out all the toonies and places them in her bag. She repeats the process with the loonies. Then she starts picking out the quarters. She is taking them out in fours. When the quarters are gone she starts in on the dimes and nickels. When she stops there is maybe thirty-five cents left in the case. She hurries off diagonally across the street without saying anything and without looking back. She disappears into an alley at the back of the parking lot.

I play only a few more songs, my energy flagging. I am intensely hungry and thinking about the coffee shop. I pack up and walk a block to where I left my car. As I am loading my guitar I see the girl walking up the sidewalk toward me. She is with a man at least three times her age. He is tall and his clothes hang loosely on his body. His face looks caved in on itself and there is a bandanna wrapped around his head.

The girl and the man walk right by but seem not to notice me. There is an energy in their movements. All of their attention is on something in the man's hand. They duck into a little garden between the sidewalk and a church. They look around, turn their backs to the street and move deeper into the shadows.

I had a sinking feeling as I walked back to the coffee shop. I lived in Vancouver's Downtown Eastside for years in the late eighties and early nineties, and I worked in the criminal justice system for over thirty years. I'm not naive. But this transaction involved me directly. Take what you need, I had said, and she took me up on it. I think it was her age and the cold calculation with which this girl had taken the money that got to me. Having witnessed the actual result of the transaction I couldn't tell myself she had bought a bus ticket home to her worried mother waiting with apple pie on a porch swing. People were dying—are still dying—every day from what they purchase on the street and put into their bodies. What was my part in this, my responsibility? I didn't taste the food I ate at the coffee shop.

I held onto this feeling for a while. Several weeks later I was talking to a friend. He asked how the trip was going. I felt a need to share the experience in Sudbury and told him what happened. His response was "Yeah, Sudbury has always had a seedy underbelly." Nothing more. No need to lose any sleep.

But a few days later I told the same story to my niece, a woman in her twenties. I must have conveyed some of my misgivings as I did so. Her response was "Just think of all the things she didn't have to do that day to get her fix." That made me feel a little better, though still not a hundred percent.

A month later I was on the return leg of my trip, cutting across central Ontario to get to Sault Sainte Marie before starting the long stretch along Lake Superior's north shore. As I got closer to Sudbury I thought about the elfin girl again, so I took the turn-off from the highway and headed for the downtown core. I didn't have a plan; I just thought I might set up and play and maybe I would see the girl again and know that she was at least still alive.

I parked downtown again, amidst the squat, concrete office buildings festooned with No Loitering signs. Within fifty feet of where I stopped a man lay unconscious beside the sidewalk. I watched him for what seemed like far too long before I could tell he was breathing. While I was watching, another man walked by, emaciated, a Naloxone kit clipped to each pant leg, swinging in time with each stride.

As I stepped from my car I was approached by a different man. He asked if I had any coins I could spare. He was young, polite, soft spoken. There was a large open wound running down the bridge of his nose. It looked infected. As we spoke, murky fluid would from time to time trickle down the side of his nose and across his cheek. He would wipe this away with his hand, like you would brush away a fly, and wipe his hand on his jeans. I gave him everything I had in my pocket, which wasn't much.

I got back in my car. I wanted to write about this, about what downtown Sudbury looks and feels like to an outsider. I had just pulled out my notebook when a woman walked up to the car and asked if I had any spare change. She was bent over awkwardly, talking to me from the sidewalk through the partly open passenger side window, saying something about a fire and emergency housing. I said sure, opening the door and getting out of the driver's seat so I could retrieve some cash from my stash in the back. The woman, easily in her seventies I would guess, was wearing a loose, floral-patterned dress, cowboy hat, designer-style sunglasses and pendant earrings featuring little sombreros. Metallic gold sandals showed off toenails polished a bright pink that matched her meticulously applied lipstick.

I gave her five dollars and asked if I could ask her some questions, if she had time to talk. The woman took off her sunglasses and took a good look at me. Then we talked, standing by the car in the weak spring sun as the other denizens of downtown Sudbury passed by. We talked about housing, the fire in her apartment building and the dark story of revenge behind it, tent cities and what happens to the bodies found therein, opioids, alcohol (the difference between being dry and being sober), recovery, work, status. We talked a lot about trauma.

When I think of this woman now, I think of her by her name, because after a good long while she held out her hand and introduced herself. I shook her hand and met her eyes and told her my name. She laughed and said, "You look like a Philip!" Then we said goodbye.

I got back in my car, once again intent on making some notes about this conversation so I wouldn't forget it. I had just settled into the driver's seat when a man came up to my window and asked for some money. It crossed my mind he must have been watching and waiting for my last conversation to end.

I never did get set up to play. I'd had enough. I didn't see the girl who, a month earlier, had taken everything from my guitar case, and I couldn't see how anyone could survive in this environment for long. I hoped she had moved on.

Before I left Sudbury, I went back to the coffee shop I had been to on my first visit. I love this place. The exterior is featureless, tucked into the ground-floor corner of a drab, four-storey commercial building. But walking into the café you have the sense of entering a small conservatory. The place is filled to bursting with plants, fed by the light from floor-to-ceiling windows on two sides of the shop. The coffee and food are excellent (I tasted it this time), and the people working behind the counter engage you warmly. The contrast with the world right outside is startling, but the café is not blind to that world. There are no signs prohibiting the use of the café's washrooms by non-customers. If you want to use the washroom, customer or not, you have to ask a barista, who accompanies you to the washroom and unlocks it for you. The barista does this gently, respectfully, and on returning behind the counter, keeps quiet tabs on the washroom door. The owners of this café have created an oasis, a small, life-affirming place, without judgment.

Wagon Wheel

In the heart of the Toronto business district the towers loom over me, as if leaning in. There is a small square of sky visible if I look straight up.

I'm in the middle of a song when a man and a woman pass by, slowing to read the sign. They stop, listening and waiting.

"Do I know you?" the man asks when I finish. "I feel like I know you."

They are a couple in their thirties, wearing worn, practical clothing against the cool weather, the man in a heavy grey wool sweater, his partner a dark purple coat with a black scarf. The man is wearing a small backpack and the woman carries a denim bag over her shoulder. There is something immediately reassuring about them, a gentle confidence in themselves.

I look closely at the man, wondering at how we might know each other, but I don't recognize him or his partner. I tell the man I don't think we've met; I'm from Nelson. He asks if he would know my music, so I tell him about First After the Fire, the band I played in, and our album, but no bells are ringing for either of us. Still, we keep talking. The man's partner waits patiently.

The man asks, "Do you know 'Wagon Wheel'?" Inwardly, I groan. Everyone knows "Wagon Wheel," even those who don't think they know it. I have previously rejected it as a cover song precisely for that reason.

But I don't want to sound like a snob. I say, "It's a pretty popular song. I could probably find the chords, but I don't know any words beyond the chorus." This is true, and I figure I'm off the hook.

The man says, "Okay, well you play it and I'll sing it. It's G, D, E minor, C."

I play the progression a couple of times. He listens, and offers, "Okay, instead of playing it *Dat*/da-da-da-da-da-da *dat*/da-da-da-da-da-da, play it *Da*/da-da/*da*-da/*da*-da *dat*/da-da/*da*-da/*da*-da." He is air-guitaring to demonstrate. I try it and get it right away.

He says, "One more thing. On the first progression you play E minor and C, then on the next you play a double C, and just keep alternating. Sorry, I forgot that."

So off I go, and I'm doing pretty well, I think, with the rhythm and the tempo. The man takes off his backpack and puts it on the ground beside us and after two bars starts in. And he's fully committed, every part of his thick, compact body moving with every word. His voice sounds as if it were made for the song, deep and rough and road-weary. It's pouring out of him into the street, up to the skyscrapers and that small patch of sky. Now I'm playing even better, feeling the song as he throws it out like a challenge, like a blessing. I join in singing on the chorus, trying not to get in the way but still flubbing a few words, and he is oblivious to my faults and carries the momentum into the second verse. When we get to an instrumental break I wish I could come up with a solo, but I focus only on keeping the groove and that works. We double up on the chorus at the end and the woman joins in with a harmony. She sounds like an angel. We are our own audience.

We come out of the song as if released from a spell. The financial district still surrounds us, going about its business. We bump fists and say our goodbyes and the man and the woman carry on.

I feel different about "Wagon Wheel" now.

In hindsight, I suppose, I must have looked pretty approachable—an older guy, playing guitar and singing home-grown folk songs, fronted by a friendly sign. At the time, though, especially at the start of the trip, it came as a surprise to me when people would walk up and want to talk. This doesn't happen to me in other contexts; I'm an introvert, and it shows, so people don't usually start up conversations with me.

But people want to talk, and music is such an easy introduction. People would ask about the meaning of a song I had sung, or if I knew a particular song (usually I did, but not how to play it), or they'd ask about my guitar, or the sign, and we'd go from there. Why is it that some of our best conversations are with complete strangers?

I got pretty picky about where I set up. Conventional busking wisdom is that the most lucrative place to play is near the exit of a liquor store, the theory being that the busker's open case offers an immediate opportunity to assuage any feelings of self-indulgence felt by those carrying their bags of liquid booty from the shop. But I couldn't bring myself to test this wisdom. It just felt too obvious, and I was looking for the broadest cross-section of people that was possible. I wanted foot traffic, and lots of it. I wanted visibility, sight lines that gave people a chance to read the sign as they approached, that gave them time to reflect, but I didn't want to be obtrusive or in anyone's way. Nobody likes to have to step around a busker. I needed something, a wall, a building, a boarded-up door, something solid behind me so I didn't have to worry about my back. And, if possible, I needed cover from the weather if it was bad. Finally, if it was available, I wanted whatever structure that was behind me to be helpful acoustically, to project my voice and guitar if at all possible. There is so much sound on the street. It's an indistinct, constant roar, punctuated by the recognizable sounds of traffic, the trucks, the buses, the construction down the block, the road crew tearing up the intersection. Against all this my voice and quiet acoustic guitar were no competition. Any kind of amplification helped.

I'd try to play between 11:00 a.m. and 2:00 p.m., when people were most likely to be out getting some food, running errands or stretching their legs. I'd scout the downtown core of the city I was in beforehand, looking for spots with potential. The prime spots were closed businesses whose front doors were recessed a few feet from the front display windows. The little alcove thus formed a sort of stage to frame me and help push my music out. With my guitar case and sign at the edge of the sidewalk, it was a space I could control, and though visible, be out of people's way. Some of these businesses even had a step or two up from the street to a small landing before the front door. This was rock star territory.

It helped if the sidewalk was very wide or if there were areas for people to hang out nearby. The vast majority of people who passed me as I was playing didn't stop. But some did, especially if there was a space within earshot that they could occupy, leaning against a building or sitting down. Not everyone on the street is heading somewhere on a tight schedule. Some have a few minutes to spare; some have more. Some are on the street all day, killing time. The busker presents a diversion, a curiosity, and to some, more.

Very few people, I found, were comfortable standing directly in front of me if they wanted to stop and listen. They'd find a spot off to the side, sometimes facing the sidewalk and street as I did. I felt a strange togetherness in this, and they'd often come up to me before leaving, thanking me for the music and leaving some coins.

I recall one person who bucked this trend. One cold day I was playing on Bloor Street in Toronto immediately beside a subway station exit. In most respects it was not the greatest spot to play, but it was sunny and there was regular foot traffic in and out of the station. I was playing "It's Not Broken," a blue-grassy, tongue-in-cheek love song where I play a solo and other stretches on harmonica along with the guitar. A woman strode from the station out to the sidewalk. Early forties, groomed to the hilt. Expensive boots and coat. Calfskin gloves. Three steps past me she turned and faced me, squarely, a bemused smile playing across her face. Unlike most people, she didn't look away. She kept her eyes unwaveringly on mine, like a challenge. And I took it. I was not going to be the one to look away, and I sang my heart out on the song. She stayed for the whole thing, until the last note on the harmonica faded into the city's dull roar. Then she gave me a full smile, turned on her heel and, head up, walked away.

I'm still wondering, *What was* that?

AM Radio

In Toronto I am set up at Yonge and Bloor, in a corner next to the entrance to the subway and shopping. There is a constant flow of people on foot. For one hour in the middle of the day, the sun finds a gap through the skyscrapers to this spot, keeping my hands warm enough to play.

Despite the traffic and construction, there are moments when the din quiets and I can hear my voice reaching the opposite side of the street. I milk these for all they are worth, proclaiming my presence in the maelstrom of the intersection.

A man walks up to me from the side. He walks behind my guitar case and sign, seemingly unaware of any boundary, actual or conventional. He is barrel chested, deeply tanned, wearing sunglasses dark enough to hide his eyes. His thick, blond hair is combed straight back off his forehead to his shoulders. There is a red bandanna around his neck and he wears a green baseball jacket, tan pants and running shoes. In the palm of one hand, held horizontally at chest level, the man is carrying an AM transistor radio, its chrome antenna extended before him. The cutting edge of miniaturization in the '70s. Music emanates.

"Can you play 'Layla'?" he asks.

I tell him I know the song, and I like Clapton's acoustic version best, but I don't know all the lyrics or how to play it.

"That's too bad," he says. He pauses. "Can I actually take something—is this for real?"

I explain the sign.

"I need two dollars for a beer. I get paid tonight, though."

I say there is no explanation needed for taking some money, wondering where you could possibly get a beer for two dollars.

"I feel like it would be stealing from you though, like it would be a crime."

I tell the man the money is not for me and the sign gives him permission to take money, so it wouldn't be stealing. People give money knowing it will go to someone else.

The man waits, looking out at the street and occasionally at the coins in the guitar case. He continues to stand close, the two of us side by side facing out from the corner. He is having a hard time accepting that the money isn't for me so I explain my motivation and the concept behind the performance.

"I guess I don't really need a beer," he says. "I'd like one, though."

I tell him he doesn't have to justify anything.

"But should I take two dollars? Do you think I should?"

"That's up to you," I say.

This goes on for some time, until at one point the man takes a toonie from the case and resumes his position beside me. The man's radio is still pushing out a mix of talk and music. For some reason I'm still strumming chords. The man continues to talk and our conversation drifts, at times pausing as we look out on the street. He mentions he was a bricklayer for twelve years until he started drinking.

He says the mother of his child —that's how he refers to her—kicked him out. I ask about his child.

"She's six. I don't see her. Her mother has her set up with her parents—she calls them Momma and Poppa."

This man, I see now, has a wealth of faint scars on his face, beneath the tan. His brows, visible from the side behind the sunglasses, are thickened like a prizefighter's. I tell him that at some point his daughter may want to meet him despite her mother's wishes, and this might be something he could focus on.

More time passes. The man, without comment, flips the toonie back into the case. A few minutes later he starts to walk off. As he passes in front of the guitar case he looks at me.

"I put it back."

"I know. I saw that."

He wanders off up Yonge Street, now holding the radio close to his ear.

The sign always drew people's attention; I could see them reading it as they walked by. Most people didn't stop or leave money. But for some, the reaction was immediate and they came right to the case while delving in their pockets. Others stopped for a bit before giving. Some walked by, stopped and came back. There were even people who passed, apparently ignoring or declining the sign's invitation, but later, as they passed again in the opposite direction, would leave some money.

It took some time for me to fully understand what my sign was asking of people. To those who might give money, it asked them to trust that it meant what it said, that it wasn't a crafty scam designed to prey on the soft-hearted. People had to trust that I wasn't pocketing everything at the end of the day, and to trust that those who took money from the case truly needed it. They had to be willing to believe their contribution would actually be helping someone, either on the street or in Europe. I tried to give back, to say thank you and to give a smile to everyone who left money. I was grateful for the cash, but more for their trust, and their willingness to pull their thoughts away from everything else, even for a moment.

Behind the sign was me, singing and playing. The sign was really just an extension of that, a neat summary of the idea I was trying to put out through my presence and the music. The sign was there to inform, but I think the music was the heart of the invitation. Standing on a street corner and playing your own songs is an act of profound vulnerability. It brings a feeling of complete exposure. Every time I opened my guitar case to set up on the street, even with no one around, I felt nervous. Each time I wondered what I was doing. I suppose the performance could be looked at as simply a part of an exchange, an offering to those inclined to leave money, or a means of evaluating the sincerity of the invitation to give or take. But I think each performance by a singer-songwriter is also an act of trust, a step into the unknown, because the singer-songwriter is sharing their feelings, trusting that their songs might be worth something to someone.

People taking money from the case, or thinking about it, were in the toughest position, I think. The word on the sign, *take*, is a crude word, loaded with stigma. It's a not-so-distant cousin to *steal*. In hindsight I prefer the idea of *receiving* rather than *taking*, but this is a fine distinction and, to me, the word *receive* carries some religious overtones. I thought using it on the sign would have been confusing. So *take* it was. The people taking money from the case had to trust they would not be judged, that their need would not be scrutinized, or just not care. I think most people did care, though. I saw a lot of people who were obviously thinking about taking money but didn't follow through, perhaps feeling shame or embarrassment. And the vast majority of those who did take money were careful, like wildebeest approaching a watering hole, first confirming the meaning of the sign and then still asking permission, and giving thanks.

Of course, some didn't care how they looked. A woman in St. John, walking by with a friend, saw the sign and exclaimed *"Take?* Hell yeah!" as she filled her pockets and walked off. But most who took money weren't like this.

In the end I decided that the sign and the music, the performance, invited an extension of trust from all three participants in the dynamic—the musician, the giver and the taker. It invited a willingness to believe in the good proposed by the sign.

That fellow at Yonge and Bloor, however, who started off asking for a Clapton tune, turned the whole thing into something else.

Metro

I am singing with a mask on, as required. It's the standard blue paper one, disposable. And everyone else within the De L'Église Metro station, coming and going to and from the trains, wears a mask too, as required.

It is mid-day on a sunny spring Saturday in Montreal. I am set up at the spot designated for busking, in the cavernous main entrance to the station, surrounded by large glass windows and concrete. The high ceiling is domed and the acoustics are heavenly. My guitar and my voice, even with the mask on, reverberate within this space, extending and mixing the notes. After weeks on the street, it is a luxury to be able to listen to myself as I play.

From the doors to my right a randomly timed trickle of people enter the station. From the stairs and escalators to my left, people from the trains arrive in waves spaced eleven minutes apart.

An hour goes by without anyone leaving anything. It's my first day in this city, and I'm starting to wonder if the apparent indifference of the commuters is just the way it is here.

In the plaza area just outside the main entrance a large group of people are variously sitting or lying on the sun-warmed ground. They are smoking, drinking and openly using other drugs. Several are stuporous or passed out, but most of the group are enjoying each other's company, talking and laughing loud enough for me to hear from within the station as people open the doors. A guitar is being passed around the group outside but no one is playing much beyond a few strums. Occasionally I hear and see one of the group calling out from the ground to people walking through their midst. I can see the eyes-straight-ahead strategy of the commuters, and wonder if their discomfort and desire to move quickly through this ad hoc party explains why no one is slowing as they pass me in the station.

I reserved this spot online. For two hours it's mine, so I keep on, playing for myself, playing for the music and the joy of the acoustics of this location, looking out at the people as they pass. As time goes on it seems people are showing more interest, pausing, listening, making eye contact. A woman walking from the train platform comes directly to me without hesitation, and puts a twenty-dollar bill in the case. A man wanders into the station from outside and stands about twenty-five feet away looking out through the windows. He stays there for over an hour, drinking, eating and even smoking, mask pulled under his chin all the while. Another man stands still about twelve feet away, directly in front of me, looking off in another direction for four songs.

I am singing my last song, "Demons." A man enters the station and reads the sign, comes closer, takes a few steps away, waits, and turns. I put everything I have into the song, hoping to draw a final donation. He waits until I finish and approaches as I am packing up. "Beautiful music," he says, but doesn't leave any coins.

"Thanks."

"I read the sign," he says. "It's an interesting idea." I think he is talking about the opportunity for people to take money, but he's got something else on his mind. He's thin, likely in his thirties, dark-skinned with short dark hair and a three-day beard. He's wearing a dark wool duffle coat, jeans, and worn, black leather shoes.

"Are you in favour of Ukraine?"

I see where he's going. "This is not about who is responsible," I say. "It's about helping people who are suffering because of the war."

That's not enough for him, though. "The media lies about the war and who is causing this violence," he says.

So we talk, and there is no invasion and it is the West and the Ukrainian government who have brought suffering on the people of Ukraine and the government controls the media for its own gain and there is no virus, no pandemic on this earth, it's all a conspiracy of the powerful to control the masses, and on it goes. There is a dark intensity to this man and somehow at the same time a compassionate acceptance of my ignorance. I am struggling to keep up with everything he is saying so I listen and ask questions and we introduce ourselves and soon we know enough about each other to want to find some common ground and we do, talking about the late spring and the warmth of the sun that is now shining outside.

What I recall most about this session in Montreal, apart from the encounter at the end, is what happened once I stopped paying attention to the party outside and stopped thinking about why no one was leaving any money. When I decided to just enjoy the acoustics of the space and lean into the music, something changed. People passing by started listening, paying attention, giving money.

Years ago I was learning to sing with a small group of musical neophytes like myself, people who loved singing but had no formal training and no experience actually performing in front of other people. Our coach was a young, accomplished singer-songwriter with boundless supportive enthusiasm and energy. At the start of the program we each picked a song to sing lead on, and our coach helped us put the songs together, guiding the lead singer with the melody and crafting harmony parts for the others. After eight weeks of working on our songs we put on a concert, backed by a band of professional musicians pulled in by our coach. It was a rush—a scary but exciting step well outside of each member of the group's comfort zone. We were stepping out of the shower and becoming performers.

I was fascinated by what happens in a live performance and why it is so different from recorded music, and I began to wonder why some live performances, even if technically flawed, are so powerful they leave you, the audience, speechless, while others don't. I remember asking our coach about this, saying something clumsy like "Why do some performances just move you so much and others don't? Like, how do you get that as a musician?"

Her answer: "When you find out, would you please let me know?"

I'm not sure I've found out the answer to this question, but I've got some theories. Ultimately, I think it has to do with the performer's motivation. Why are they singing? What is their purpose? Is it money, fame, recognition? Are they just passing time?

To me, the most moving performances are those where the singer is actually not performing at all, but rather is simply connecting fully with the song. They are feeling it as they play. This is a palpable thing for both the singer and the audience, undeniable when it happens. There is a connection, a sharing of space, some kind of exchange of understanding. Both singer and audience are caught up in what the song is saying. This only happens if the singer lets go of themself and whatever else is weighing on their mind and plays with an open heart, for no other reason than to express what they are feeling. Open heart begets open heart, and an audience can't help but be drawn in.

Josh Ritter wrote a song, "Snow Is Gone," which asks us to go easy on someone who sings for adulation. Applause is the most seductive and, ultimately, self-defeating type of motivation. I believe an audience can tell immediately when there is an ulterior motive behind a performance. In even the tiniest nuances it is perceived, and a sensitive audience can't reciprocate with the open heart that permits understanding of the unique expression of feeling in the song. In the long run the musician will be cynical and miserable, because once hooked on applause there is never enough.

When a musician is intent on only the *feeling* of the song, it doesn't matter if there is one or a thousand people listening. For the performer there is only the complete, mindless focus, the immersion in present feeling. It's a meditation that others can join.

It's not easy, though. There are so many distractions! And the idea of publicly displaying one's feelings in the moment takes real courage. It can take a lifetime of practice. But I believe those moments of complete immersion, rare though they may be, are the life-blood of performing musicians, whether they are onstage at Carnegie Hall or in the De L'Église Metro station in Montreal.

Fredericton and St. John

In Fredericton there is a man playing saxophone at the only likely busking spot, the downtown mall. The man is walking around as he's playing, looking bored and distracted. I go for a walk. When I come back forty-five minutes later, the man is gone.

The spot feels exposed and characterless, a concrete walkway against a drab stucco wall beside the mall entrance. All of the city buses, maybe eight in total, arrive simultaneously from their respective routes. They idle for ten minutes in their prescribed, angled slots along the side of the building then pull out together, as if on a military exercise.

When the buses aren't coming and idling and going, it's quiet. The lunch hour is over and many of the shops in the mall are closed. I wonder if this is because it is Monday or whether they are businesses that went under during the pandemic. There is an open Starbucks by the mall entrance, though, which helps.

People walk by, reading the sign. A few leave money, but no one slows or lingers.

A man in a grubby unzipped parka yells at me from across the street. He has the dark, weathered face and rough beard of someone who lives outdoors. His long, greying hair is suspended by its natural unguents in every direction about his face. He could be forty or seventy. He starts across the street toward me, stopping halfway to yell again. It sounds like, "Are you using standard tuning?"—a question I take as intended to convey he is a musician. He is carrying some sort of odd electronic instrument under one arm, a bulky, square platform partly hidden by his parka. It doesn't look like a keyboard, but there are knobs and dials and some strings showing. On he comes, unstable to the point of staggering. In an almost unintelligibly slurred voice he says, "Don't worry, I'm not drunk." Though he's still ten feet away I can smell the alcohol pouring out of him.

I don't offer any invitation or encouragement, but the man puts his instrument on the ground and places himself right beside me against the stucco wall as if we are old friends or bandmates. My strategy is to ignore him and hope he'll go away. With a glazed stare broken by slow blinks, he watches me play "Similkameen." It feels like his face is right in mine, and I can smell much more than alcohol now. I feel like a contestant in some sort of bizarre game or contest of wills.

Out of nowhere, the man joins in and sings a few notes. They are the right notes. I realize he hasn't been staring, he's been listening. But he can't continue, can't maintain that focus. It was there, though, and I realize he is indeed a musician, and he knows enough not to continue if he can't follow the music.

I get to the end of the song and the man is having trouble standing. The spot is so barren; there is nowhere to sit other than the concrete walkway or quartz gravel border along the building. He mumbles that he is going to find something to sit on and starts to move off. He is so pie-eyed I'm not keen on him returning. He has left his instrument on the ground and I ask him if he wants to take it with him. Either he gets the hint or he has just enough continuing awareness to know he is in no shape to enhance anything I am doing. He says, "I'll move on." I can hear the resignation in his voice, and I think about that, though I don't object.

A week later, I am playing outside the downtown market in St. John, singing my last song at the end of a sunny lunch hour. A young woman crosses the street to me and waits. There is another young person with her, pushing a kid's scooter. When I finish the song the young woman says, "Excuse me, could I ask you a question?" I say sure.

"Would you happen to have a few coins you could spare me? I'm seventeen and I've been kicked out by my foster parent."

The young woman is neatly dressed, clear-eyed, direct and polite. She has a Tim Hortons cup in her hand with a few quarters in it. She tells me she has been in the system since she was five and doesn't know her parents. The person behind her, standing with one foot on the scooter, doesn't speak. I can't tell their gender. They are wearing a toque under a bike helmet that sits off-kilter. They are looking away from our conversation but don't seem to be in any hurry.

I say to the young woman, "So, you must have a social worker?"

"She's on holiday, so I called the on-call worker who's meeting me with the police at five o'clock." All said without hesitation.

I ask, "Well, what's going on with your foster parent? Do you think you could get back in there?"

"He raped me." Again without hesitation, matter-of-fact.

"Okay... that's why you're meeting with the police at five?"

"Yes."

I absorb all this for a bit but can't really think of what else to say that might help. I ask her, "Have you read the sign?"

"No." She steps in front of the sign and reads it.

"What does this mean?" she asks.

"I'm playing music. People can leave money if they feel like it, or take money if they feel they need it. Anything that's left goes to Ukraine relief."

There is one five-dollar bill in the guitar case and maybe ten dollars in change.

"Would I be able to take five dollars?"

"Of course."

She takes the bill. "Thank you very much," she says, and they head off.

———————————————————————

By the time I busked in St. John I had already reached Halifax and spent an afternoon playing in a sunny spot along the harbour walk, much as I did in Nanaimo near the start of the trip. I felt pretty buoyant about having reached the other side of the country. At one point I toyed with the idea of extending the trip to Newfoundland but, with my available time ticking away and the cost of putting my car on a ferry to the island, I decided to head back.

As I drove west toward home I was continuing to busk in places I'd missed on the way out. It felt different on the way back, though. It was harder to stay motivated. At times during this trip I felt tired, or hungry, or cold, or all three. My fingers would freeze during some sessions. The couple of times I actually camped I was so uncomfortable on my half-length Therm-a-Rest, and so cold, I slept only in short, shallow snatches, emerging from my tent in the morning bleary-eyed and sore everywhere. Some of the motels I stayed at (much cheaper than the cheapest Airbnb) were pretty awful. In many of them I slept in my sleeping bag on top of the bed, a precaution I began to take after pulling back the sheets at one place and not liking what I saw. And much of the time I was lonely, going entire days with only a few words to another human. At times I wondered what the hell I was doing and felt sorry for myself.

Busking sessions like these ones in New Brunswick, however, usually straightened me out.

Hot Dogs

The Hudson's Bay building in Winnipeg, built in 1926, closed to the public in 2020 because the store was no longer profitable. Due to the cost of necessary renovations, the market value of the property was estimated at zero. At a ceremony in April 2022, with the prime minister present, the Hudson's Bay Company gave the building to the Southern Chiefs' Organization, an agency representing thirty-four First Nations in southern Manitoba. There are plans to redevelop the structure with social housing, business space and restaurants. For now, the building remains locked and boarded up.

These are facts I heard on the radio as I drove eastward across the prairies on the first leg of my trip, watching the frozen land unfold and running through snowy squalls that obliterated everything. Now, on my return trip weeks later, I am walking in the wind and cold rain of downtown Winnipeg, and I see the building I'd heard about on the radio. It is massive, occupying an entire downtown block. At Portage Avenue and Vaughan Street, an overhang wraps around the curved corner of the building and a recessed alcove precedes double doors into the main floor. Cigarette butts cover the tiled floor of this entrance, and the space smells of urine, but the overhang and the alcove afford shelter and an excellent vantage onto the intersection. A Tim Hortons across the street and bus stops on two corners ensure foot traffic on this Saturday morning, despite the weather. It's the best spot I can find to play.

I set up in the alcove entrance, my guitar case and sign, as usual, just in front of me, protected by the overhang. The traffic noise, amplified by the wet streets, ebbs and flows in a slow rhythm dictated by the lights at the intersection. I am grateful for the way the cave-like space behind me projects the sound of my guitar and voice during the brief intervals of relative quiet.

I am a white male, sixty years old, wearing a black watch-cap toque, charcoal grey wool jacket, new Wranglers and Merrell running shoes.

It's not busy. I am mostly playing to myself and watching the street. People pass, heads down, protecting themselves from the weather. The buses come and go. I see an Indigenous man in a wheelchair across the street, stationed outside the entrance to the Tim Hortons. A white woman comes out and puts a tall cup in his hands.

I play for a while, and eventually a man on an electric mobility scooter crosses the street and stops by my case. He is white and in his sixties. His left leg is a gleaming metal prosthetic. A husky wearing a service dog vest walks beside the man's scooter, attached by a six-foot leash. The man drops some coins in the case and says hello, then says, "Well, let's hear something." I play a song, and from the way the man listens and watches my fingers for the chord changes I can tell he is a musician. When I finish the song he introduces himself as Rick and tells me he's been playing for forty-five years. We talk about busking and how a good song is timeless. The dog has been scanning the street continuously and becomes impatient to go. Rick wishes me well and drives off.

I resume playing. Across the street there are now several people sitting on benches near the Tim Hortons entrance. I see two people walk up the sidewalk and approach them. The two people are handing out items from large plastic bags. One of the people, a man, crosses the street to where I am playing. He is white, mid-fifties, sporting a silver brush cut and wearing a clean grey sweatshirt and jeans. Brush Cut addresses me as I'm playing: "How are you doing today?" He wears a benevolent smile. I stop singing, but keep playing.

I say, "Just great, thanks, how are you?"

He says, "Wonderful. Could you use some food?" Without waiting for an answer, Brush Cut presses something he has extracted from one of his bags into my chest. I am compelled to stop playing and take his offering. It is two foil-wrapped tubes. They sit warmly in my cold hands.

"Are these hot dogs?" I ask.

"Yes!"

"Are they meat hot dogs?"

"Yes!" Even brighter.

I decline the man's offering, apologizing as I do, but accept the bottle of water he also presses on me. Brush Cut moves on.

Shortly after this exchange, a different man, one I hadn't yet noticed, walks quickly into the alcove behind me. He is carrying a hot dog in each hand, still in their foil wrappers. His face is partly obscured by a Covid mask and a hoodie, but I can see the man is white, likely mid-thirties.

Hoodie seems not to notice me as he shuffles about the alcove, occasionally squatting to sift through the cigarette butts. I am playing chords but not singing because I am half-turned into the darkness of the alcove, watching him.

After a while Hoodie comes up to me, close, and begins to talk. With his mask on and the sound of traffic reverberating in the alcove it is hard to hear him, but what I do catch makes little sense. He is talking about five hundred people being killed, he is talking about a hammer, he is talking about his sister. I cannot trace the connections. He asks me questions with insistent intensity, but to me they are just unconnected words with a question mark at the end.

I tell Hoodie I can't understand what he is saying and he turns away in evident frustration. He leans against the corner of the entrance to the alcove, opens one of the foil tubes, pulls his mask under his chin and starts picking apart the hot dog with his fingers. It's just a plain hot dog, without mustard or anything else, in a soggy white Kleenex bun. I start playing again, but I stop when Hoodie steps toward me holding a steaming chunk of dull pink hot dog meat between his thumb and index finger and asks if he should put it in my guitar case. This question I understand.

I say, "No, thank you." I give him the plastic bottle of water and start singing again, hoping he will go away. But he doesn't. He returns to the corner he was leaning against, about four feet to my left, and looks out on the street.

Now another man, young, white, wearing a ball cap, crosses Portage Avenue to the corner I'm playing on. Ball Cap bends and places coins in the case. I'm in the middle of a song but break away from the lyrics to thank him. As Ball Cap is turning to leave, Hoodie, still with the hot dog in his fingers, addresses him. Ball Cap pulls closer, trying to understand. I can see him struggling, as I did. I hear Ball Cap say, "I'm just a fellow soul on this planet...", but he is then interrupted by a stream of opaque questions from Hoodie. Eventually it seems Ball Cap concludes it is possible Hoodie is asking for money. Ball Cap points toward my sign, saying to the other man, "You just have to read the sign, and that will solve your problem." Hoodie doesn't even follow Ball Cap's motion. He continues his unintelligible speech. Ball Cap looks over to me. I give him a short, rueful smile and a nod, and he leaves.

The Indigenous man I had seen at the start in the wheelchair outside the Tim Hortons rolls across the street. Wheelchair still has the large coffee cup, as well as two still-unwrapped hot dogs in his lap. I say hello but he doesn't answer. Wheelchair is a large man with shaggy hair low on his brow, maybe in his late forties. His right leg ends above the knee. His grey sweatpants are tied in a knot below the stump.

Hoodie has remained at the entrance to the alcove and resumed picking apart his hot dog. Wheelchair rolls by him and spins the chair behind my guitar case. Now he is immediately beside me, also facing the street. He does not acknowledge me in any way.

I move a bit to the side to create some space, even though it feels I am abandoning my position directly behind the guitar case. I carry on singing and playing. Wheelchair is listening, his foot tapping the concrete in time. Hoodie is now moving, once again roaming around the recesses of the alcove.

Wheelchair suddenly starts talking loudly, yelling actually, as I try to play. He rolls away from the case and intercepts Hoodie deep in the alcove. Wheelchair screams at him, telling the man he is going to kill him, lunging. I hear some sort of contact, an impact, and Hoodie walks quickly, stiff-leggedly, out of the alcove, around the corner and out of sight. He has left a half-eaten hot dog on the ground.

Wheelchair is quiet again and rolls back, but now slightly behind me. When he sees three young women in police cadet uniforms heading into the coffee shop on the opposite corner, he starts talking again. Beyond the anger in his voice, I can't understand much. He's going on about the police and the IPs, which I take to refer to the Indian Posse, a Winnipeg street gang. I don't know what to say to Wheelchair, but he is quickly ramping up as he did before, getting louder and louder, now beyond shouting, to the point of incoherence. His hands are in his lap, clenching and unclenching.

I don't want to run from this man, but it's just him and me. I'm looking at him, talking quietly, trying to demonstrate some empathy, but it crosses my mind that I have become the source or at least the focus of his rage.

I can think of nothing more to say than "I hear you, I

hear you," over and over, as I kneel before him to pack up my guitar. He is still screaming as I leave.

I realize that spot never was mine.

Winnipeg in early spring is harsh. In that time when the white blanket of winter has receded but it is still so cold that the trees and other plants do not have the courage to let loose their buds, the city is naked and grey. There is trash everywhere. It's mostly fast food packaging—paper wrappers, take-away boxes, cups, plastic lids and straws, and loads and loads of plastic bags. There is no lack of garbage cans. They are everywhere too, all empty, surrounded by the sea of what has been pulled from them. As they are filled they are emptied onto the ground so their contents can be known. Anything of any value, like a pop can, is quickly picked up.

The city's core is cold, the side streets lined with dilapidated houses, every third one abandoned by its owners, derelict. Doors and windows are smashed. Some of these are covered by blankets or sheets or even Canadian flags tacked up by those that shelter within. Early one morning I watched a ragged man walking down the middle of one of these streets. He was carrying a cordless drill before him like a toy gun. There was still enough charge in the battery to work the tool, and the man's face was filled with delight as he pulled the trigger for short bursts while he walked.

The joy and diversion of an easily liquidated power tool aside, it felt to me, a visitor, as if the suffering in this place was pervasive, and accompanied by the threat of hair-triggered, desperate violence.

In any city buskers are in a vulnerable situation on the street, especially if they are strangers to the area. There may be unwritten local rules and unmarked territorial boundaries they won't know. They may have cash openly displayed before them, which makes them a potential target, even with a sign such as mine. With a guitar around one's neck defence is difficult if it becomes necessary. The most a busker can do is to find a spot from which to see any trouble approaching, to read the street, and to be prepared to leave before things go south.

⅄

In Winnipeg I stayed in an Airbnb, a small, old house in the city's core, a couple of blocks off Portage Avenue where I busked. The house has been renovated and tastefully decorated by the owner, who lives there. This youngish man rents out the two bedrooms on the second floor, just down the hall from his own. There is one bathroom. While you are staying there you are treated as a roommate, not a guest. The host is himself, clearly comfortable having you living with him. There is no awkwardness. I could have happily stayed for more than the couple of nights I was there, but I'd been on the road for six weeks by then and was feeling the pull of home. On the morning I left, my host and I sat on his front stoop, drinking coffee, enjoying the sounds of returning birds and the thin, barely warm sun reaching through the naked branches of the lone tree in front of the house.

Police Lake

I was in Calgary, striking distance from home.

For a few days I stayed with my friend Vern at his condominium. I worked with Vern years ago as a prosecutor in the Okanagan, and it had been years since I'd been in touch with him. His fifteenth-floor condo sits on the edge of the downtown core, neatly fitted between the skyscrapers and the Bow River. There are expansive views in three directions. The bed in Vern's spare room was the most comfortable I'd been in for almost two months. We were making meals in the open, well-stocked kitchen and eating like kings. It felt a bit surreal after the previous seven weeks of mostly dodgy motels and dormitory-style Airbnbs, of inconsistent food, of driving all day, playing on street corners and carrying on.

I busked a couple of times along the river walkway, but mostly I hung out with Vern. It felt strange to be around another person, the same person, for long stretches of time. Vern comes from a Ukrainian family. The war, then just three months old, dominated his thoughts and many of our conversations. He would stay up late each night pouring through online sources, feeding on the latest information. He was reading everything, from mainstream media sites to tweets from soldiers on the front lines.

I was homesick, but not quite ready to go home. As I saw the end of the trip approaching, it all started catching up with me, all the distance, the sights, the people, the weather, the hard nights and constant change. I was feeling numb and disorganized. It had been great to spend time with Vern, but it was nothing if not intense—not just because of the contrast in comfort, but because of the depth and breadth of our conversations.

At some point while crossing the country I had told myself that before returning to Nelson I would spend a few quiet days on my own hiking and camping somewhere. Despite the pull of home, I resolved to follow through on this plan, to give myself some time alone to reflect on the previous two months.

Police Outpost Provincial Park seemed the perfect place to do this. It's a remote park tucked into the southwest corner of Alberta, nestled against the American border to the south and the Rockies to the west, about a three-hour drive from Calgary. The land there is rolling grassland with small pockets of aspen, wild rose and saskatoon bush. The area is dotted with small bodies of water, and the lake in the park is the largest of these. To those not from the southern prairies it might look like nothing more than a large pond, but Police Lake is stocked with trout so that, despite its remoteness, the park is a popular camping spot. I'm not crazy about car camping in provincial parks, but I'd been to Police Outpost years ago at the end of one summer and had fallen for its windswept openness. I could see myself walking all day on the rolling plain, feeling exposed to the sky all around, the imposing, tusk-like shape of Chief Mountain jutting up in the distance just over the American border. Then I'd cook a meal and write a bit before falling asleep with the sounds of the wilderness around me.

Unwind. Take a deep breath. It seemed the perfect way to end the trip before driving the last leg home.

Police Outpost also happened to be the only provincial park open in the entire province of Alberta on the May long weekend. I went to the government website to reserve a campsite for a couple of nights and found there was only one remaining available site. It seemed everyone was keen to start the camping season. I had hoped it wouldn't be so, that I would have the place to myself, but I remembered having a spot with some privacy the last time I'd been there, so I snagged the last site.

I left Vern and the shiny city and drove south, straight down Highway 2. The drive was uneventful. It was cool and overcast, but dry. The traffic on the four-lane divided highway was steady. As I had many times over the previous weeks, I wondered where everyone was going, and how many intricate stories I was surrounded by, separated only by a few feet of asphalt and the steel and glass casings of our vehicles as we hurtled through the open land. I was still caught up in the energy of the last few days. I'd had more conversation in that time than I'd had in the previous two months. I felt unsettled, socially overdosed. My mind was whirling through it all, not stopping anywhere, unable to slow down.

In Cardston, the last town before leaving the highway, I gassed up and bought two large bottles of water and some fruit. I had enough food to get through a few days.

After turning off the highway the road surface soon turned from asphalt to gravel and clay. I'd forgotten how long that part of the drive is, and how much the land rises as you continue southwest toward the mountains. The land rolls higher and higher as you get closer, as if the mountains are pushing back against the carpet of the prairie, lifting it. What had been a uniformly overcast day began to look more ominous as dark, heavy clouds loomed over the road. The land became snow-covered as it rose before me. There were no other vehicles in the final stretch to the park.

I was almost expecting the gate to the park to be closed and locked, but it wasn't. As I drove through and around the campsite loop, I could see only a few trailers in their slots. There were three or four at most. I reasoned that it was early, only four in the afternoon, and everyone must still be on their way. My campsite, Number 16, was sandwiched tightly between its neighbouring sites, with little in the way of trees or other vegetation separating them. It was the usual rough gravel pad with a picnic table and steel firepit. An outhouse was directly across the road-way. There was no running water. I pulled in and got out of the car just as snow pellets began to shoot down as if from a gun. I breathed in and was shocked at how cold it was.

Fire is the thing, I told myself, and walked down to the firewood bin at the entrance. It was empty. Whoever had opened up the park for the weekend had not brought any wood for the campers, contrary to the assurances of the booking website. I walked back to my site and started setting up my tent, the snow still driving down, beating a staccato on the roof of my car and the tent fly as I stretched it over the arced pole frame. Once the tent was up, I threw in my Therm-a-Rest, sleeping bag and the one blanket I had brought with me.

The snow squall ended and I set up my gas camping stove. I cooked some dehydrated backpacking curry and some tea. Everything was coated in snow and ice and there wasn't really anywhere comfortable to sit other than the car, so that's where I ended up, sitting in the front passenger seat spooning the orange muck into myself. Something tasted off in the curry.

It was still early, with hours of light left in the day. After cleaning my bowl, spoon and the cooking pot I decided to go for a walk. I headed for the lake and took the trail along its shore. After ten minutes walking I turned off the main trail onto the boardwalk that bridges the shore to a small island. I leaned against the rail, looking into the wind over the lake to the mountains to the west. Chief Mountain stood apart from the rest, a massive loner. It and the wall of mountains beyond were grey, indistinct, virtually featureless as they rose out of the land. They were simply part of the continuum linking the ground to the sky, all of it veiled in cloud and falling snow, all of it cast in black and white and grey. The wind off the mountains began to come in heavier gusts, scudding across the lake, punctuating the bleakness.

I kept walking. For some reason I couldn't get warm, even though I was moving continuously as I navigated the trail. The path stopped abruptly about a third of the way around, so I decided to bushwhack from there, pushing my way through the tangle of short trees and brush fringing the lake and climbing up to the bare ridge above it. After another half hour I'd made it all the way around and headed back to my campsite.

As I walked through the loop toward my site I could see that most of the sites were still empty. At my site, however, two trucks towing sizeable campers had pulled into the two spots above mine, each with its own family. The families clearly knew each other and were in the process of settling in and setting up one double-sized camping compound. I listened to the two fathers barking commands at the older kids like drill sergeants, clearly enjoying their position of superior car-camping experience. Their wives looked after the babies and toddlers, bundling them up, moving in and out of the campers as they got dinner going. The families had brought their own firewood and their firepit was already sending up serious flames. I counted nine children between the two groups, thirteen in all with the adults. No one acknowledged my presence as I puttered around my site, putting away my stove and moving my water into the tent in the hope it wouldn't freeze overnight. I said hello to one of the fathers but only received a less than enthusiastic "Hi" in return before he turned away to direct more orders at one of the kids. There would be no neighbourly banter. The light was starting to wane. I decided to go to bed.

For some people, camping in a provincial park is primarily an opportunity, once everything is set up, dinner is done and the kids are all tucked into their beds in the trailer, to sit with friends around an open fire, drinking and talking late into the night. My neighbours were these kind of people. The four adults were at it until two in the morning. The wind had died with the sun and through the crystal clear mountain air every cheesy country pop song from their portable stereo, every click and gaseous burst from every freshly opened can, every word, laugh, grunt and fart of their little wilderness party entered my tent. I was, after all, only twenty feet away.

After the party died there was a short period of silence before a dog on the other side of the loop began barking. He or she kept it up for an hour, and I lay there wondering how its owner could possibly let it go on. I was fighting for sleep, in and out of it by then. I was wearing long underwear, socks and a toque, and I'd pulled the hood of my three-season sleeping bag tight around my head, but it got colder and colder as the night went on. I had to pee, and for a long time I fought it, not wanting to leave what little warmth I had. But the need to go only grew and eventually won this battle. I unzipped everything and crawled out onto the snow-covered gravel, pulled on my boots and stumbled to the back of the campsite to find a dark tree to urinate against, enjoying the relief while at the same time wishing it wasn't taking so long because of the biting cold.

I returned to the tent and tried to salvage some sleep from what was left of the night, but now was more awake than ever. There was another brief period of absolute silence, and then I became aware of a regular, intermittent drumming. It came up from the ground under my tent, through the makeshift pillow I'd fashioned from a rolled-up jacket. I could feel it, the pressure of it, in my body. At first I wondered if it was coming from some camper's sound system, or whether I had fallen into some kind of sleep-deprived auditory hallucination. But there was something familiar about the rapid, insistent repetitions, the unrelenting resonance through the earth. I'd heard that sound before when camping in the mountains early in the year: the spring drumming display of the ruffed grouse.

I lay for another hour, still thinking I might get some rest. It seemed to be getting lighter in the tent. I checked my phone. It was five in the morning. I quit fighting for it and got up.

In the half-light outside the tent all was still. Only the grouse, still intermittently thrumming away, disturbed the icy quiet. I got the stove going to make coffee and oatmeal. The raspberries I'd bought the day before had frozen hard overnight so I stirred them into the hot porridge. I cupped my hands around the rapidly cooling mug of coffee and ate standing up, moving my feet to keep circulation going.

I finished eating the last of the oatmeal and scraped up some snow to clean the pot. I was feeling strangely nauseated and, taking stock, realized I was also sore, tired and weak. At some point in the night I had already decided that if the weather didn't change I wouldn't stay another night as planned. But suddenly the weather wasn't even a factor. The pull to get home that had slowly built over the last couple of weeks had suddenly become an imperative. I had to get home that day. I packed up and drove off, the sun just up, still no one stirring among the few occupied sites in the campground.

I don't remember much of the drive home, north from the park to Highway 3, then west past the Frank Slide and through the Crowsnest Pass into the East Kootenay, there following the Elk River for a long stretch, then through Cranbrook and Creston, over the Kootenay Pass to Salmo and finally north up Highway 6's narrow valley to Nelson. Normally a six-and-a-half-hour drive, it took me almost ten, all pretty much a blur. I was so tired I kept having to stop for fear of falling asleep at the wheel. I'd pull over and lean the seat back, doze a bit, get out and walk around still feeling dizzy and on the verge of vomiting, then get back in the car and continue until I had to stop again. I remember also, as I got closer and closer to home, how lush and green the forest verging the road seemed by contrast to everywhere I'd been for the last two months.

Finally I pulled into my driveway. I was greeted by Dana and our dog, Emmet, but it wasn't the lengthy, joyous return I had envisioned, because I went straight to bed. It was four-thirty in the afternoon and I didn't get out of bed for another day and a half. I had bouts of fever through that time but tested negative for Covid. Regardless, something had hit me hard.

And that was that, the spectacularly dismal end to my trip.

Small Things

- The woman in Vancouver, tall, stylishly dressed, wearing oversized sunglasses, who read my sign from the other side of Homer Street as she waited with the other pedestrians. When the light changed, the woman stepped outside the white lines of the crosswalk and made a beeline toward me. She put a ten-dollar bill in my guitar case then looked at me squarely and said, "Thank you for doing this. I am Ukrainian. Are you Ukrainian?" I told her I wasn't, but I had a sister who lived in France who was taking in Ukrainian families fleeing the war, and I was trying to help out too. I could see the woman's eyes behind the shade of her glasses, and there was a moment where nothing was said, but we shared a sense of sorrow, injustice and compassion. We thanked each other simultaneously and she walked off.

- The man with the topknot at the Sherbrooke Metro station in Montreal who dropped coins in my case as he walked by, getting about thirty feet past me before returning, fishing in his pocket, and adding a five-dollar bill. Then he went to the ATM by the pay entrance to the trains.

- The five schoolgirls on a bright lunch hour in Kingston, young teenagers moving excitedly as a group, a continuous flurry of light-speed interactions. One happened to read the sign as they passed and, while they waited for the light at the corner, turned, came back, placed coins in the case and returned to her friends. A number of them then looked back, also reading the sign. One of them came back to leave coins, quickly followed by another who left a five-dollar bill. Then on they went, reassembled, faces into the spring sun.

- The boy, maybe fourteen, heading for the street from the train at the Sherbrooke Metro station. He was walking quickly, but slowed and stopped in front of the sign. He removed his bulky backpack and placed it on the concrete floor of the hallway as the crowd of other people coming from the train parted and passed around him like a stream around a rock. The boy knelt and rummaged in his pack, finally digging out a granola bar, which he placed in the case. He looked up and smiled.

- The young male cop crossing the street in Saskatoon who looked me in the eye, smiled and gave a thumbs-up.

- The elderly woman walking carefully by on a grim, windy day in Toronto. She wore a long wool coat with a silk kerchief knotted under her chin. The woman stopped and delved into her handbag, bringing out a small, embroidered change purse. With black-gloved fingers she unsnapped the purse and fished about, then held her fingers like talons over the guitar case, letting the coins fall, some of them pennies.

• The two young men in Charlottetown who threw coins in the case and stopped to talk. One wore a Montreal Canadiens ball cap. "Away Guy," I said in my best French-Canadian accent, referring to Lafleur, who had died the previous week, and who at one time was the best hockey player in the world. "Yes, away Guy," the young man replied, with the same reverence.

• The teen wearing a rainbow mask in Saskatoon who suddenly appeared from between angle-parked cars with a five-dollar bill ready in her hand. She shyly tucked it under some change in the case, and when I said, "Thank you very much," she said, "Thank *you*."

• The woman who heard me singing the chorus on "Demons" as she approached within the wave of just off-loaded Metro commuters. She picked up on the melody right away and added a wordless harmony, her voice floating above the crowd in the concrete tunnel, entwining with mine as she passed.

• The sad-looking man wearing a baseball cap in Saskatoon who heard me playing from across the street and came to sit on the bench about fifteen feet away. He sat, completely still, holding his gaze away from me but listening intently. I could see him tapping his foot. I had about five songs left in the set and I decided to banter about them. He turned and looked as I talked and sang. At the end I thanked him for listening and spending the time with me. He looked like he wanted to say something, but couldn't. So we just looked at each other.

- The woman, walking with a friend along the Bow River walkway in Calgary. They walked by and were almost out of my peripheral vision when the woman stopped and walked back to me while her friend waited. The woman was in her fifties, wearing an expensive coat and boots—a competent, busy person. She thrust her fist at me, palm down, commanding, "Put this away." I didn't understand, and she repeated herself. I held my open hand below her fist, and she dropped a crumpled fifty-dollar bill into it. I started gushing, wanting her to know her trust was justified, but she was already walking away.

- The woman in her hijab in St. John, with her rambunctious kids. "I love that," she said to me, referring to the sign. She recorded part of "Zephyr" on her phone and left some coins.

- All of the preschoolers, out with their moms or dads or other caregivers, bursting with cautious excitement as they approached the strange man singing and playing guitar on the street or waterfront, holding chubby hands out to drop a precious coin into the guitar case—no less magical than a wishing well—to join the other shiny treasure scattered across the green, furry interior, then turned and ran back to safety, only to ask for another coin so they could do it again.

- Everyone who had enough courage and trust to take what they needed.

After

Life goes on. In hindsight, it was naive to have thought that a few days camping and hiking at the end of the trip would be enough to allow me to process the previous two months. In the weeks after I returned to Nelson, friends and others would ask me how the trip went. "How was it?" they'd ask. I didn't know how to answer this. I would say it was interesting, or something about how cold it was. I had collected just under two thousand dollars, most of it in quarters and loonies, for the Red Cross's Ukraine Humanitarian Relief program, so I'd tell people about that when they asked. I couldn't answer questions about how much was taken from the case by people on the street because I hadn't kept track.

It felt like nothing I could say, though, could adequately describe the experience. People seemed to want to know if it was a "success," by which I think they were curious about whether I had found what I was looking for, whether my reasons for taking the trip, whatever they were, were addressed. But not having had a specific set of goals or expectations going into the trip I was without a metric by which to gauge it in that way.

Just before I started the trip a friend encouraged me to write a few pages every day, to write without thinking, "morning pages" style. I think she sensed I was looking for some resolution of where I was in the wake of a lengthy, intense career, and thought that writing during the trip might result in some helpful insights about myself and my changing place in the world. It had been years since I had done any consistent journaling, but I followed through on my friend's suggestion and did write, almost every day of the trip. I'd write while pulled over somewhere in my car, or in a coffee shop, or wherever I happened to be staying. Some of it was indeed the kind of writing suggested, letting whatever emotion I was feeling or thought I was having spill out onto the page. But most of it was about what happened on the street as I was busking. This wasn't a conscious choice; it just happened that most of the time I was writing I found myself trying to set down, as accurately as possible, what I had seen and heard while playing.

Months after I was home in Nelson, I pulled out the Moleskine notebooks I had taken with me on the trip. What jumped out at me when I looked at the pages of rapid scrawl were the people on the street who had wandered by or stayed for a time as I played, those who somehow got pulled into the session for whatever reason—maybe the music, maybe the premise and intent behind the sign, maybe just boredom or curiosity. These were more than interesting to me. The notes became the busking stories that have made their way into this book, and I have done my best to tell them exactly as they happened.

Did I find any insights about myself in those notes? Not immediately. It can take a while to understand how a new experience has shaped your thinking and how you see the world. Mostly I think we change without knowing it.

But as I began to write these stories and think more about the trip, I made a few discoveries.

A small one: I am now far less self-conscious when playing and singing than I was before the trip. That's hardly a surprise, though. Keep pushing through and the path gets easier.

Another: this country, vast though it is, seems smaller now. The fact that you can drive from one side to the other and back, gas stop by gas stop, every mile of it passing before your eyes, and on one set of worn-out winter tires, makes it seem more finite to me. And, by extension, the world also now seems smaller.

I know, too, that in the wake of the trip I have a renewed sense of the privilege I have in this world—privilege that, to the extent it is the result of the skin, gender and stable family I was born into, is unearned. I try not to forget this.

I've found that I can't think about the trip without thinking about the decision to leave my legal career. The two are interwoven. It was the decision to leave my job that spawned the idea of busking across the country and, once in my head, this idea persisted and sustained me through the remaining months of work and then the months that followed as I began to figure out life after judging and waited for the world to open up.

At the time I decided to leave judging I told myself, and others, that I knew I was making the right decision. At least part of saying that was an effort to bolster myself, to thwart the fear I had. Back to the cliff-jumping analogy.

You may not even know exactly why you are doing it, and at the moment you jump you don't know for sure how it's going to turn out. Whatever the thrill or other reward you may have anticipated leaves some room for potential disaster. All that is left after the leap are the consequences. There is no appeal process; you take what you get. Part of what I got after that gloomy November night in Nelson when I sent my resignation email was the busking trip.

As it was for many people, the pandemic was the catalyst for me to start thinking about making a change in my life. I think most of us now, consciously or unconsciously, avoid dwelling on those two surreal years of Covid. We refer to them in our conversations, but often only obliquely. We don't talk about them much. Like a lot of songwriters, I wrote a song about the pandemic while it was happening. But I haven't heard many people sing their pandemic songs, and I have never sung mine publicly. People don't want to be reminded. It's too fresh. If I make myself think back to the feelings of those years it becomes almost overwhelming. Every day of the pandemic forced the realization that nothing is secure, that life is fragile and uncertain, that nothing can be taken for granted.

It was this realization that drove my Covid reckoning, that and the sudden deaths of a number of friends and acquaintances, people who were about the same age as me, and like me, assumed they had many years left to do all the things they wanted to do while here. They left a lot on the table.

The pandemic also brought a recognition of how much I had been missing. There was a specific moment this was brought home. When the pandemic closed all the schools, my eldest son came home from university in Victoria. His last classes and final exams for the year were online. After his last exam I asked him if he knew what courses he would be taking in the next term, and he told me he'd just finished his degree after five years of study. I was stunned. In my mind he had only been away at school for a few years, maybe three at most. Such had been the focus on my work over the previous years.

Judging is an extraordinary job. Every day is different and there is no end to the learning. The pay and benefits are good and you always have a parking spot. But the core of the job is the opportunity it presents to resolve conflicts in a way that the people involved can understand and respect, and thus help them move along with their lives. That's the satisfying part of it, and I loved that part.

Like any job, judging has its good days and bad days, days when it seems you are doing some good and others that are filled with frustration. It can also be heartbreaking. People and their life stories pass before you continuously, many of them sadder than you can imagine, and just when you think you've heard the saddest story of all time, a sadder one comes along. The work demands a constant awareness and measuring of your emotions to ensure they are not interfering with the task you have—making decisions based on reason and law established by legislation and precedent.

In the first couple of years of judging the learning curve is steep. I wasn't surprised that the work essentially took over my life during that time. I thought this would change over time but it didn't. As the years rolled on, I found that though the learning curve had become less steep, the work continued to consume most of my life. Part of this was simply because of the volume. The hours were long, and as I mentioned early in this book, I often found myself working late and on weekends. As a judge I was never quite comfortable, never without some self-doubt. I told myself this was a good thing, because the moment the job felt easy would be the moment I was in danger of missing something and making a mistake. But I never learned the knack of leaving work behind when I left the courthouse. The evidence and issues raised by cases remained in my mind, churning away. It became a pattern for them to surface at three in the morning. I'd wake up and they would swim about in my head for hours. Eventually I stopped trying to get back to sleep when this happened because the answer, or the right path to the answer, would often come to me at those times.

Music was an outlet, a reprieve from the work, and I squeezed it into any spare moment I had. But it felt like there was never enough room for it, and there was virtually no room for anything else.

It's amazing what you can get used to. It took the pandemic to make me realize two things. The first was that the job of judging would not change for me. The approach I took to it was the only one I knew and was part of my nature. I wasn't capable of finding a healthy balance. So long as I continued to do it, the work would continue to be all-consuming. The second realization seems so obvious as to be trite, but I think many of us refuse to face it nonetheless: time is limited, and potentially much more limited than you think.

So, after living with these realizations for some time, I did what I was trained to do. I weighed the evidence, applied the relevant principles and arrived at an answer. The answer I came up with was that I could reasonably expect ten to fifteen more years of good health, if I was lucky. No guarantees. Boiling it down to those numbers brought a stark realization. If I wanted to do more with my life than what I was already doing, if I wanted a different balance, I'd better get on with it.

The pandemic continued as I finished my last day in court, and in some ways things were getting uglier. We had watched on January 6, 2021, as the United States Capitol Building was attacked by a mob intent on keeping Trump in power. A year later, in our own country, a trucker convoy protesting gas prices and Covid health mandates took over the streets of downtown Ottawa. People were tired, angry and intolerant. Our differences, be they over politics or vaccines (and these became co-mingled) were running deeper. It seemed to me we weren't listening to each other anymore. Facts and science didn't matter except when they supported our personal beliefs— beliefs that to me seemed to be mostly about what we wanted, not what was true. Increasingly, social media was becoming a weapon instead of a connection. And at times it seemed the world itself was turning against us as the effects of climate change ramped up. In my home province of BC we were dealing with heat domes, massive floods and forest fires.

I was busy through that time, throwing myself into as much as I could in the newness of not judging, but the weight of it all was getting to me. Through the winter of 2021–22, I wondered: *What is happening to us?*

Then, on February 24, 2022, Russia invaded Ukraine, and the atrocities of that war, which continue to this day, began. It was impossible to absorb. The busking trip across Canada, put off now for months, was still constantly on my mind. I planned to start out as soon as I could. I didn't know what to expect of this trip in the face of all that was happening. I made the sign, packed up the Honda Fit and set out.

⋏

The sign wasn't entirely truthful, I now realize. As I pulled the stories out of my notebooks and revisited the thoughts I had recorded during the trip it became obvious. I hadn't been playing for fun. Although I didn't recognize it at the time, beneath the desire for adventure, for doing something I'd never done before, and for getting out on the road to see the country after two years of limited travel, there was something else—a need for reassurance. I needed to know that despite our failings, our poor responses to the challenges of the world, there is another, enduring side to us, a side that has the capacity to close the gaps between us and offer something selflessly, even to someone we'll never see.

And it was there. Over and over. From the teenager in Montreal who placed a granola bar in my case to the woman in Calgary who dropped the fifty-dollar bill in my hand, that other side was there. I was just a guy on the street with a homemade-looking sign playing songs no one could recognize, and still people were willing to jump in, to trust the opportunity that was being offered and respond with kindness. By the same token, others were willing to trust the intent of the sign and the performance enough to take money from the case, and almost without exception they did so with honour and gratitude.

These small things, these moments, reminders of what we can be, are what this journey became for me.

So yes, life goes on, and it has. I'm still trying to find the right balance, to grow and learn, and to serve others in some way. I write and play music when I can. The busking trip, born of a decision to move on from a career, has stayed with me.

Busking, I've learned, is both an expression of trust and an invitation. The busker, like any musical performer, asks the question: "Do you feel this too?"

It can be hard work. I don't pass by any busker now without at least some form of acknowledgment—even, if I have no cash, just a word or a smile. Something to let them know, "Yes, I feel that too."

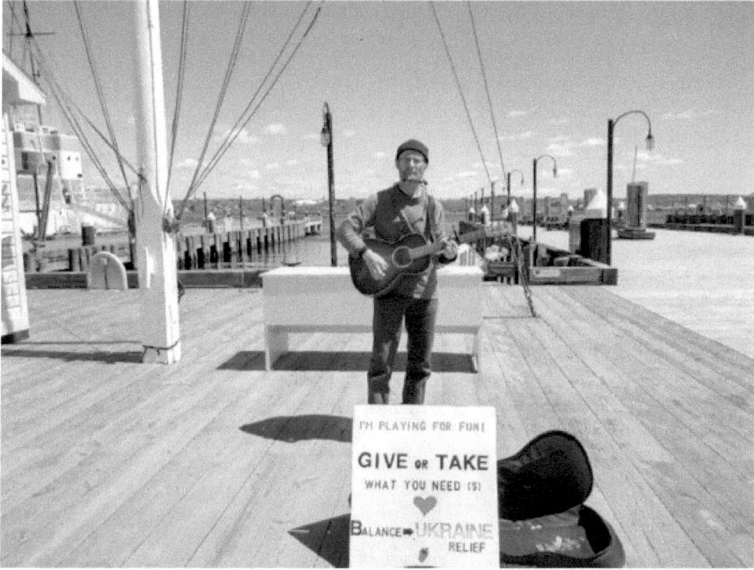

Halifax harbour, May 6, 2022

Acknowledgments

I am lucky to have been able to share some of the first stories and early drafts of this book with a number of smart, generous people. Without their input and encouragement the book would never have come to be. I am grateful for the always frank and varied comments of my Taghum Hall writing group—Melodie Rae Storey, Keitha Patton, Elenna Hope, Ron Butler and Liz Amaral—as well as for the helpful suggestions of my friends Carrie Clark and Carlo Alcos. I am particularly thankful for the unfailingly helpful advice of my friend and mentor Anne DeGrace who, more than anyone else, made me believe *No Judgment* might be worth putting out there. And then there is the constant support of my wife, Dana—my first and best reader.

Finally, thanks to the crew at Caitlin Press for their belief in this work.

About the Author

Philip Seagram is a former criminal lawyer and provincial court judge who has lived and worked in Vancouver's Downtown Eastside, the Okanagan/Similkameen, and the West Kootenay. Now a late-blooming singer-songwriter, writer, and cross-country ski instructor, he lives with his wife, two horses, a dog and a cat on a small acreage near Nelson, BC.